Planet
Earth

CHRISTINE TAYLOR-BUTLER

Children's Press®
An Imprint of Scholastic Inc.
New York Toronto London Auckland Sydney
Mexico City New Delhi Hong Kong
Danbury, Connecticut

Content Consultant
Bryan C. Dunne
Assistant Chair, Assistant Professor, Department of Astronomy
University of Illinois at Urbana–Champaign
Urbana, Illinois

Library of Congress Cataloging-in-Publication Data
Taylor-Butler, Christine.
 Planet Earth / by Christine Taylor-Butler.
  pages cm. — (A true book)
 Includes bibliographical references and index.
 ISBN 978-0-531-21150-2 (lib. bdg.) — ISBN 978-0-531-25356-4 (pbk.)
 1. Earth—Juvenile literature. I. Title.
 QB631.4.T395 2014
 525—dc23   2013023429

All rights reserved. Published in 2014 by Children's Press, an imprint of Scholastic Inc.
Printed in China 62
SCHOLASTIC, CHILDREN'S PRESS, A TRUE BOOK™, and associated logos are trademarks and/or registered trademarks of Scholastic Inc.

1 2 3 4 5 6 7 8 9 10 R 23 22 21 20 19 18 17 16 15 14

Front cover: Illustration of a comet passing Earth
Back cover: Astronaut Edward White performing a space walk

Find the Truth!

Everything you are about to read is true *except* for one of the sentences on this page.

Which one is **TRUE**?

T or F Earth's magnetic north pole will eventually shift to the South Pole.

T or F Humans have explored 75 percent of Earth's oceans.

Find the answers in this book.

Contents

Meteor showers take place when small objects from space burn up in Earth's atmosphere.

The *Aqua* satellite carries six instruments to study Earth's water cycle.

CHAPTER 1

The Blue Marble

Have you ever wondered why life exists on Earth but not on other **planets** in the solar system? Earth is the third planet from the sun. If it were closer to the sun, it would be too hot to support animal or plant life. If Earth were farther away, it would be too cold. Instead, Earth contains the perfect conditions to support a variety of climates and **habitats** that make Earth's plant and animal life possible.

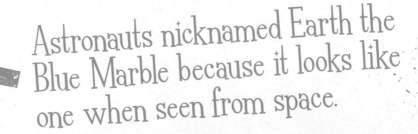

Astronauts nicknamed Earth the Blue Marble because it looks like one when seen from space.

Imperfect Sphere

Earth is the fifth-largest planet in the solar system. It looks like a ball, but its shape is not a perfect sphere. Instead, it bulges at the **equator**. If you wrapped a tape measure around the equator, it would measure about 25,000 miles (40,000 kilometers) around. It would be roughly 8,000 miles (13,000 km) in diameter, or across. What if you measured Earth's diameter between the North and South Poles? That number would be 26 miles (42 km) shorter.

Earth's name comes from the Old English and German words *eorthe* and *erda*, meaning "ground."

Earth is the third planet from the sun. Our solar system includes eight planets in all.

A Trip Around the Sun

Like other planets in our solar system, Earth orbits the sun. Earth's orbit is not a perfect circle. It is an **ellipse**. Scientists estimate that Earth is an average of 93 million miles (150 million km) from the sun. It takes 365 days and six hours to complete one revolution. An extra day is added in February every four years to make up for those extra six hours. Years with the extra day are called leap years.

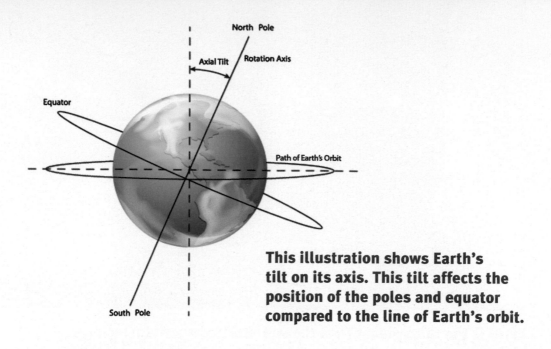

North Pole

Axial Tilt   Rotation Axis

Equator

Path of Earth's Orbit

South Pole

This illustration shows Earth's tilt on its axis. This tilt affects the position of the poles and equator compared to the line of Earth's orbit.

Spinning Like a Top

While orbiting, Earth spins like a top on an invisible axis. That axis extends through the North and South Poles. This rotation creates days on the planet. Areas facing the sun receive daylight. Those facing away experience night. One day on Earth lasts 24 hours. Our planet is divided into 24 time zones. This helps keep track of the different phases of light on Earth. See *The Big Truth* (page 22) for more information on time zones.

Earth's axis tilts 23.5 degrees as the planet orbits. This tilt causes the seasons. For six months each year, the Northern **Hemisphere** tilts toward the sun. As Earth revolves around to the other side of the sun, the Southern Hemisphere tilts toward the sun. As a result, when it is summer in one hemisphere, it is winter in the other. When it is spring in one hemisphere, it is fall in the other.

Earth travels around the sun at about 67,000 miles (108,000 km) per hour.

During summer in the Northern Hemisphere, the sun shines more directly on the Northern Hemisphere. During winter in the north, the sun shines more directly on the Southern Hemisphere.

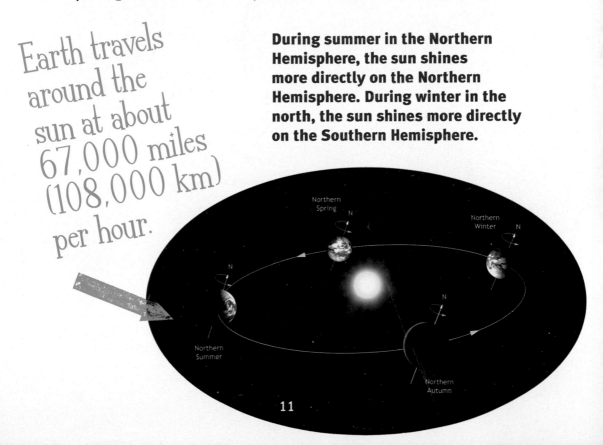

Northern Spring

Northern Winter

Northern Summer

Northern Autumn

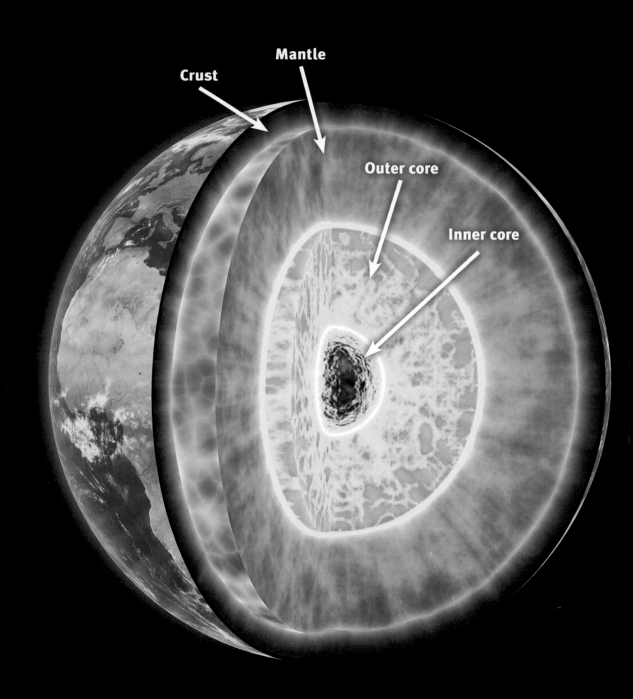

CHAPTER 2

Above and Below

Below us, our planet is composed of four main layers. The outer surface is called the crust. Beneath that are the **mantle**, outer core, and inner core. Circling overhead is a layer of gases that forms our atmosphere. Each layer plays an important part in Earth's ability to sustain life. For example, plants and animals depend on liquid water on Earth's surface to drink. As a gas, water can travel on winds to fall on places around the world as rain, snow, or hail.

 Earth is the only planet in our solar system where water exists as a solid, liquid, and gas at its surface.

The Crust

Earth's outermost layer includes the continental crust and oceanic crust. The crust and the uppermost layer of the mantle are broken into sections called **tectonic plates**. The plates rest on top of a more fluid layer of mantle and are constantly moving. Scientists believe Earth's continents were once joined as a single landmass called Pangaea. Over millions of years, the tectonic plates shifted. This caused Pangaea to break into sections. The sections drifted apart and formed the continents we know today.

Earth has seven major plates and many smaller ones.

Pangaea covered almost one-third of Earth's surface. The remaining surface was taken up by an ocean called Panthalassa.

14

Tectonic plates sliding against each other can cause mountains to rise along Earth's surface.

When tectonic plates slide over or past each other, an earthquake can occur. Sometimes the pressure causes shifts in the oceans. If the ocean earthquake is strong enough, waves can develop into a deadly tsunami.

The collision or constant pressure of tectonic plates can create mountain ranges. For example, the Himalayan mountains in Asia grow taller each year.

The movement of water is shown in blue arrows in this diagram.

Water on Earth circulates constantly through the water, or hydrologic, cycle. Liquid water on the planet's surface is heated by the sun and turns into a gas. This gas, called water vapor, rises into the atmosphere. It gathers into clouds and falls back to the ground as precipitation, such as rain or snow. It collects in bodies of water or soaks into the soil. Then it starts the process over again.

The Mantle

Earth's mantle is a semisolid and movable layer of rock. It is composed of silicon, oxygen, iron, magnesium, and aluminum. Sometimes this substance rises through the crust above. It surfaces as a volcanic eruption of **molten** rock.

Scientists believe the mantle is about 1,860 miles (2,993 km) deep. This calculation is an estimate. No one has ever drilled deeper than 1.4 miles (2.3 km) beneath the ocean or 8 miles (13 km) on land.

Islands such as the Hawaiian Islands were created as molten rock rose up from the mantle through the crust beneath the ocean.

Earth's Crust

Larger flow of magma

Earth's Mantle

The Core

Earth's core has two layers. The liquid outer core is composed mostly of iron and nickel, and is about 1,400 miles (2,250 km) thick. It is constantly flowing. Its movement around the inner core creates Earth's magnetic field. Enormous pressure and **radiation** keep this layer hot. The inner core is solid iron. It may spin faster than Earth's other layers. The whole core is estimated to be 11,000 degrees Fahrenheit (6,000 degrees Celsius).

Earth's core may be as hot as the surface of the sun.

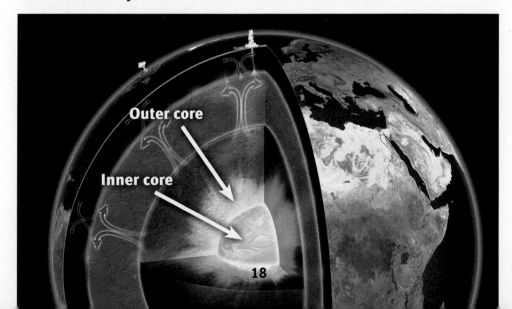

Outer core

Inner core

This illustration shows the five layers of Earth's atmosphere.

A Layer of Protection

Earth's atmosphere wraps the planet like a blanket of insulation. Its two lowest layers are the troposphere and the stratosphere. More layers of thinner and thinner air are above the stratosphere.

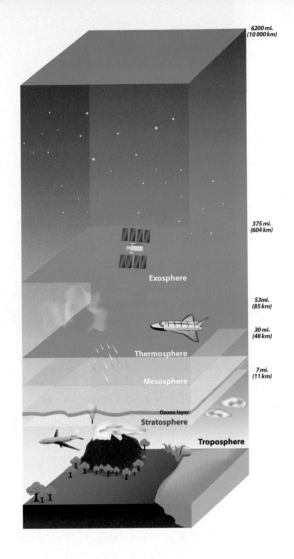

6200 mi. (10 000 km)

375 mi. (604 km)

Exosphere

53 mi. (85 km)

30 mi. (48 km)

Thermosphere

7 mi. (11 km)

Mesosphere

Ozone layer
Stratosphere

Troposphere

The troposphere is about 7 miles (11 km) high. It contains the air we breathe. It is 78 percent nitrogen, 21 percent oxygen, and 1 percent other gases. Nearly all of the weather we experience on Earth occurs in the troposphere.

Falling stars are actually meteoroids burning up in the upper atmosphere.

Meteoroids rarely make it to Earth's surface. If they do, the chance of them causing harm is very low.

The stratosphere is about 30 miles (48 km) high. It contains less water and more **ozone** than the troposphere. Ozone blocks harmful rays from the sun. The stratosphere and the layers above it also help protect us from objects in space, such as meteoroids. These objects sometimes threaten to crash into Earth. However, a meteoroid creates friction as it moves rapidly through the atmosphere. This usually causes the object to burn up.

Which Way Is North?

A compass needle points to Earth's magnetic north pole. But did you know that the magnetic north pole is not located at the geographic North Pole? The magnetic pole drifts about 6 to 25 miles (10 to 40 km) each year. The north and south magnetic poles sometimes switch places. When this happens, Earth's magnetic field temporarily becomes twisted and scrambled. But this has only happened 170 times in the last 80 million years. After the next switch, a compass needle that would have pointed north will point south.

North Pole

Magnetic field

South Pole

Dividing Time

Earth is divided into 24 standard time zones. Each time zone is one hour ahead of the zone to the west of it. For example, say it is 12 p.m. in Anchorage, Alaska. At that same moment, it is 1 p.m. in Los Angeles, California.

Most areas have adopted these standard time zones. But there are some exceptions. China crosses three standard time zones. But the country decided to have only one time zone. Some regions divide time zones by half hours. Iran, Newfoundland in Canada, and parts of Australia are examples.

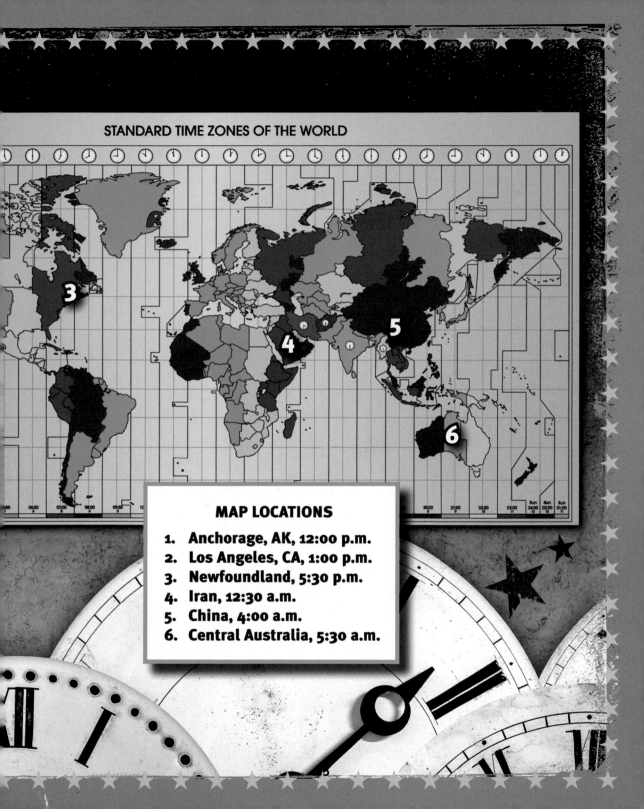

STANDARD TIME ZONES OF THE WORLD

MAP LOCATIONS

1. **Anchorage, AK, 12:00 p.m.**
2. **Los Angeles, CA, 1:00 p.m.**
3. **Newfoundland, 5:30 p.m.**
4. **Iran, 12:30 a.m.**
5. **China, 4:00 a.m.**
6. **Central Australia, 5:30 a.m.**

The same side of the moon always faces Earth.

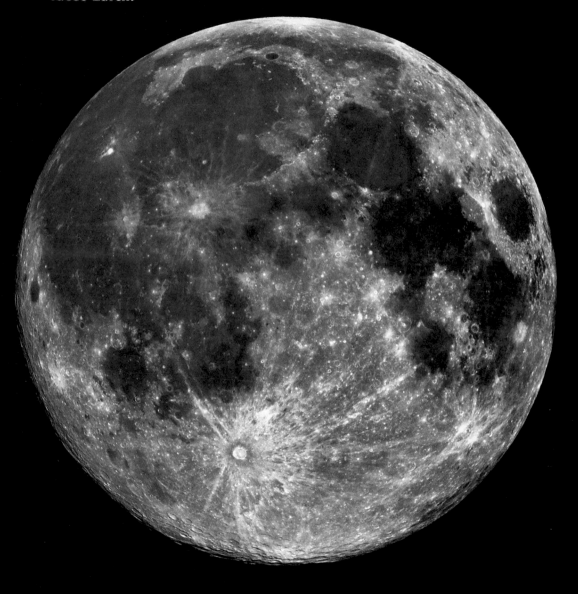

The Moon

Some planets have many moons. Others have none. Earth has only one moon. It is located an average of 238,855 miles (384,400 km) from Earth.

Earth's moon is a type of satellite. A satellite is an object that orbits another, larger object. Moons are natural satellites. That means they were not made by humans. Using this definition, Earth is a natural satellite of the sun.

The moons of other planets are each given names so they are not confused with Earth's moon.

A Helping Hand

Although the moon is a lifeless rock in space, it provides benefits to our planet. Earth's gravity pulls on the moon, but the moon's gravity also pulls on Earth. The moon's gravity causes Earth's ocean tides. They help circulate water and slow Earth's rotation. Scientists believe the moon's gravitational pull also helps keep the tilt of Earth's axis stable. This keeps our climate stable.

High and low tides follow the moon's orbit.

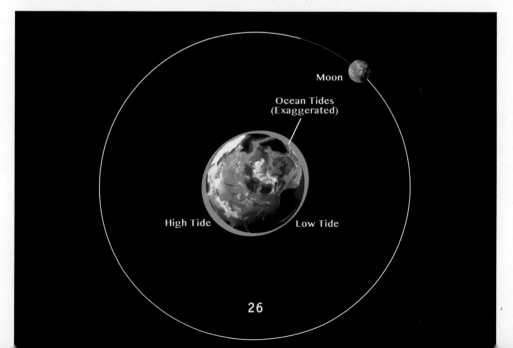

Moon

Ocean Tides
(Exaggerated)

High Tide   Low Tide

26

The moon completes one orbit around Earth every 27.3 days.

Making the Moon

So where did the moon come from? Some scientists believe that an object the size of Mars collided with Earth 4.5 billion years ago. The moon was created from molten debris flung into space by the collision. As a result, the moon's surface contains elements similar to Earth's crust.

The moon has no atmosphere. Therefore, it is not protected from space debris. Craters form when asteroids, meteoroids, and comets hit its surface.

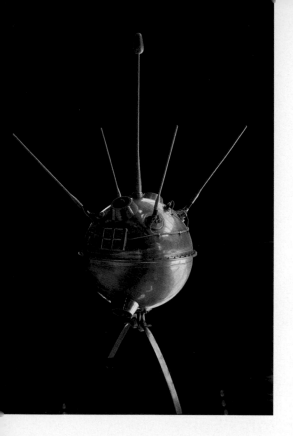

Luna 2's inventors also called the probe the "second cosmic rocket."

Exploring the Moon

The Soviet Union, which included present-day Russia and nearby countries, launched **probes** to the moon in 1959. The first probe, *Luna 1*, missed its target and orbited the sun instead. *Luna 2* crashed on the moon 33.5 hours after it launched. Its equipment detected no radiation or magnetic field.

The United States launched spacecraft to orbit the moon in 1966 and 1967. These helped map the moon's surface. The information was used to plan the first manned missions to the moon.

In July 1969, the *Apollo 11* spacecraft landed on the moon. Astronauts Neil Armstrong and Edwin "Buzz" Aldrin became the first people to walk on the moon's surface. By 1972, 10 more astronauts had repeated that journey. A total of 842 pounds (382 kilograms) of rocks was collected for study.

Exploration did not end there. In 2009, the **Lunar** Crater Observation and Sensing Satellite (LCROSS) discovered water crystals on the moon. This water could help support future manned missions there.

Neil Armstrong took this picture of Buzz Aldrin on the moon. If you look closely, you can see Armstrong's reflection in Aldrin's visor.

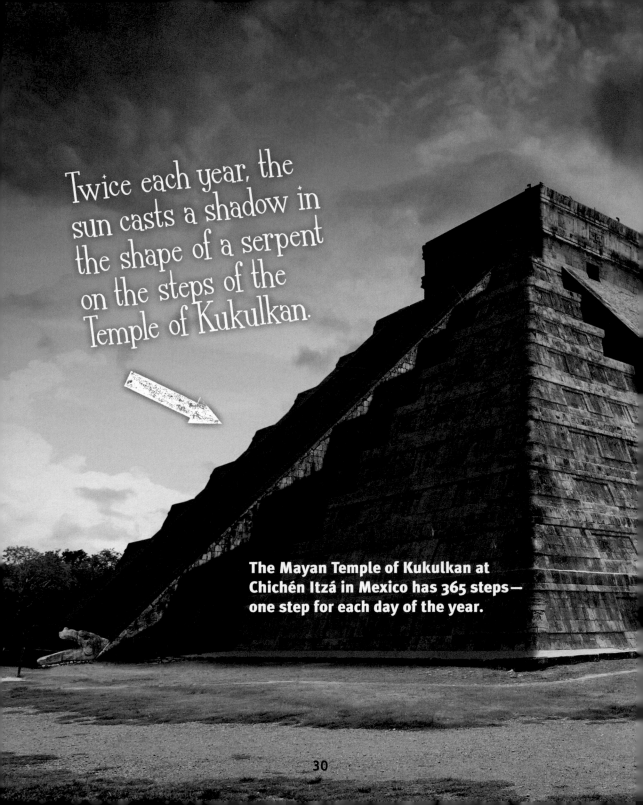

Twice each year, the sun casts a shadow in the shape of a serpent on the steps of the Temple of Kukulkan.

The Mayan Temple of Kukulkan at Chichén Itzá in Mexico has 365 steps— one step for each day of the year.

CHAPTER 4

Center of the Universe?

Ancient civilizations had many different ideas about Earth. Incan and Mayan people believed that Earth had four corners. Ancient Egyptians believed the sky was a flat plate held up by four mountains. The ancient Chinese believed the sky was a sphere surrounding a flat land. Early Greeks believed Earth was a cork floating on an ocean. Early astronomers used math and observations to learn about the planet. But many mysteries were not solved until the invention of the telescope.

Determining Shape

In 350 BCE, Greek philosopher Aristotle observed that objects always fell to the ground. This was true no matter where in his travels he dropped them. He also noticed that when ships sail over the horizon, their masts disappear last. He observed that Earth casts a round shadow on the moon during a lunar eclipse. These and other observations supported the idea that Earth is a sphere. Objects fall toward its center.

Aristotle believed that Earth's main elements were air, water, fire, and earth.

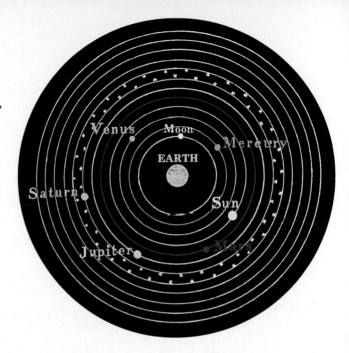

Ptolemy's theory of the universe is called geocentric. This means Earth is at the center of the universe.

Imagining the Universe

Greek astronomer Claudius Ptolemy drew a map of the solar system in 150 CE. His illustrations placed Earth at the center of the universe. Ptolemy argued that the sun, moon, Mercury, Venus, Mars, Jupiter, and Saturn orbited Earth. This was a common idea at the time. Aristotle had supported it 400 years earlier. Ptolemy also created a list of 1,000 stars. Those stars were believed to orbit Earth outside the orbit of Saturn.

Ptolemy's theories remained popular for another 1,400 years. Then, in the early 1500s, Polish astronomer Nicolaus Copernicus published a book showing the sun at the center of the universe. This new model better explained the behavior of the planets. However, the Copernican theory conflicted with the teachings of the Catholic Church. The church was very powerful at the time and banned Copernicus's book.

Timeline of Earth Exploration

350 BCE
Aristotle determines that Earth is round.

150 CE
Ptolemy publishes a map of the universe with Earth at the center.

In 1609, Italian physicist Galileo Galilei was shown a "spyglass." The spyglass, or telescope, made faraway objects appear closer. Galileo improved the design and was able to observe distant planets, moons, and other details for the first time. Galileo published his findings, stating that Copernicus's theories were correct. This and other ideas got him into trouble. In 1633, he was put on trial for disobeying the church. The court sentenced him to life under house arrest.

1609
Galileo publishes findings that support Copernicus's model of the universe.

2000
The International Space Station welcomes its first crew of scientists.

1543
Copernicus's work arguing that Earth and other planets orbit the sun is published.

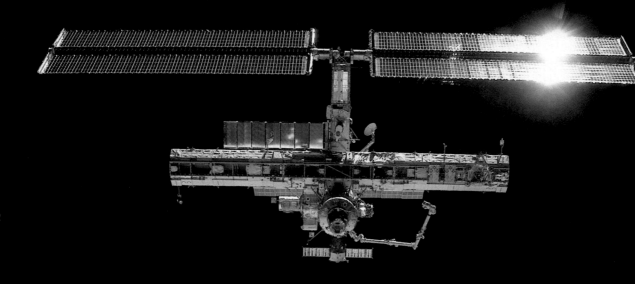

CHAPTER 5

Mission Earth

Technology has come a long way since the days of ancient astronomy. Satellites create detailed images of Earth from space. Probes deep inside the earth and in the ocean monitor the health of the planet. Global Positioning System (GPS) satellites allow us to navigate the planet without having to study the stars. Now scientists can spot problems and react quickly to natural disasters. This helps reduce the devastation the events could cause.

A GPS satellite completes one orbit around Earth every 12 hours.

The Undiscovered Deep

Oceans are one of Earth's most abundant resources. But only 5 percent of the ocean floor has been explored. That is changing. The National Oceanic and Atmospheric Administration is studying deepwater canyons off the coast of Virginia. There, they use remote operated vehicles (ROVs) and **sonar**. Woods Hole Oceanographic Institution uses a human-occupied vehicle and other underwater machines to explore and map even deeper waters. These missions help explain Earth's geologic processes.

A remote operated vehicle can dive about 21,000 feet (6,500 meters) for up to 16 hours.

The Japanese vessel *Chikyu* holds the world's record for deep-ocean drilling.

To the Center of the Earth

The exact nature of Earth's mantle is still unknown. To solve this mystery, scientists are hoping to drill directly into the mantle and take samples. Geologists plan to drill through a section of the Pacific Ocean floor estimated to be less than 4 miles (6.4 km) thick. Special drills are being designed to handle the stress of boring through the hard oceanic crust. This $1 billion project is planned to start drilling in 2020.

Mount Erebus is so popular it has its own Facebook page.

A scientist uses specialized equipment to study the crater at Mount Erebus.

Exploring Earth's Mantle Through Volcanoes

Antarctica's Mount Erebus is one of Earth's most unusual volcanoes. It is largely covered in ice. But it contains a lake of molten hot lava deep inside its crater. Scientists at the McMurdo Station research facility analyze the gas and lava produced by Mount Erebus. The data helps explain how and why volcanoes erupt. It can also tell us a lot about the mantle's chemical composition.

Destination Space

Human-made satellites also help us study Earth. The *Aqua* satellite was launched in 2002. *Aqua* uses microwave technology to see through clouds and monitor Earth's water cycle. For example, water and ice from melting polar caps could shift ocean currents. Weather would change, and Earth's temperatures could plunge. Other satellites look for activity signaling earthquakes, tsunamis, or other natural disasters. Satellites can track storms or changes in Earth's climate.

The *Aqua* satellite is a joint project between the U.S. National Aeronautics and Space Administration and Japan's National Space Development Agency.

41

To learn how things work in a weightless environment, world scientists designed the International Space Station (ISS). ISS welcomed its first astronauts on November 2, 2000. Since then, more than 200 scientists and engineers have visited the station. They have conducted more than 400 experiments. As of 2013, ISS completed more than 57,000 orbits around Earth.

Exploration continues to expand. People once thought Earth was the center of the universe. What will we discover next?

ISS orbits 240 miles (386 km) above Earth.

Where on Earth Are You?

Do you use GPS to navigate? If so, you're receiving information from the 29 GPS satellites orbiting Earth. The U.S. Air Force maintains these satellites. Twenty-four satellites are active. The other five are backups. The satellites transmit radio signals to a GPS receiver in your phone or car. Signals from four or more satellites are needed to accurately determine your position. Digital maps are built into the receiver. They use the satellites' information to help you navigate.

True Statistics

Depth of Earth's crust where it is thickest: 37 mi. (60 km), on land

Depth of Earth's crust where it is thinnest: 4 mi. (6.4 km), in the Pacific Ocean

Size of Earth's largest continent: 17 million sq. mi. (44 million sq km), Asia

Size of Earth's smallest continent: 3 million sq. mi. (8 million sq km), Australia

Size of Earth's largest ocean: 59 million sq. mi. (153 million sq km), the Pacific

Depth where Earth's ocean is deepest: 7 mi. (11 km) below sea level, at the Mariana Trench

Most active volcano on Earth: Kilauea in Hawaii

Did you find the truth?

(T) Earth's magnetic north pole will eventually shift to the South Pole.

(F) Humans have explored 75 percent of Earth's oceans.

Resources

Books

Aguilar, David A. *13 Planets: The Latest View of the Solar System*. Washington, DC: National Geographic, 2011.

Arlon, Penelope. *Planets*. New York: Scholastic, 2012.

Munsey, Lizzie. *My Tourist Guide to the Center of the Earth*. London: DK, 2013.

Visit this Scholastic Web site for more information on Earth:
★ www.factsfornow.scholastic.com
Enter the keyword **Earth**

Important Words

ellipse (i-LIPS) — a flat oval shape

equator (i-KWAY-tur) — an imaginary line around the middle of a planet or other body that is an equal distance from its north and south poles

habitats (HAB-i-tats) — places where animals or plants are usually found

hemisphere (HEM-i-sfeer) — one half of a round object, especially a planet

lunar (LOO-nur) — having to do with the moon

mantle (MAN-tuhl) — the part of Earth between the crust and the core

molten (MOHL-tuhn) — melted at a high temperature, usually describing metal or rock

ozone (OH-zone) — a form of oxygen that has a pale blue color and a strong smell

planets (PLAN-its) — large bodies orbiting a star

probes (PROHBZ) — tools or devices used to explore or examine something

radiation (ray-dee-AY-shuhn) — energy or particles given off in the form of light or heat

sonar (SOH-nar) — a device that finds objects using sound waves

tectonic plates (tek-TAH-nik PLAYTS) — huge, slowly moving sections that make up Earth's outer layer

Index

Page numbers in **bold** indicate illustrations

About the Author

Christine Taylor-Butler is the author of more than 60 books for children including the True Book series on American History and Government, Health and the Human Body, and Science Experiments. A graduate of the Massachusetts Institute of Technology, Christine holds degrees in both civil engineering and art and design. She currently lives in Kansas City, Missouri.